Foundation
-Majestic Forte-

Marcus Yates Ford

Copyright © 2019 Marcus Yates Ford
Majestic Forte All rights reserved. No part of this book may be reproduced, stored in a retrieval system or transmitted in any form or by any means without the prior written permission of the publishers, except by reviewer who may quote brief passages in a review to be printed in a newspaper, magazine, or journal

ISBN-13: 9780578495699
Published by: Majestic Forte
The MF Signature
Houston, Texas

Printed in the United States

Foundation

Dedication

Westbury Church of Christ
Vacation Bible School
The Church Retreat in Oklahoma '87

My Foundation
Matthew 7:24-25

Foundation

Create Enhance Inspire

Foundation material

I made the decision on July 31, 1987 to have the opportunity to be a future resident in heaven. I accepted Jesus Christ at 10 years old. To this day, it is my most valued decision I have ever made. This decision serves as my foundation. My foundation contains my formal education, Sunday Bible School and exposure through several aspects of learning. This book contains 87 entries that express my thoughts daily and throughout the years.

Table of Contents

Horizon

Abundant Beauty From The Cross 15
Agape 16
Best Kind of Love 17
Connection 18
Deeper Than What You See 19
Dosage of Praise 20
Enhancement 21-22
Expression 23
Foreign Land 24
Gala 25
Give 26
God made me 27
Heart 28
Highest of All Time 29
Love is Easy 30
No Ceiling 31
Out of Darkness 32
Pray to God 33
Seeds 34
Stone 35
Supportive 36
Strings in my Heart 37
The Natural Number Following 5 & Preceding 7 38
The Spirit of Sam/Sam Made me Smile 39
Three 40
Truth 41
Velocity 42
Wonderful Change 43

-

-

Table of Contents

Innovation

Abandonment 47
Allure 48-49
Back in the starting blocks 50
Basic 51
Check 52
Dish 53
Factory Rest 54
Fallback 55
Free Living 56
Karma 57
Looking Back on Vanity 58
Man with the Beard 59
My Packed Bag (Quondam Contemplation) 60
Over/Dose 61
Perceptions and Illusions 62
Prescription 63
Searching for a Signal 64
September Rest 65
Spike Lee's New Actor 66
The Path to Normality 67
Tranquility 68
Vote 69
Wait for Me 70
War of Women 71
Winter Breeze 72
Young Man 73
111.11 74
2, 4, 5 and 6 75

Table of Contents

Structure

ABillionsmiles 79
Acknowledgement 80
Fingerprints 81
Fraction 82-83
Help 84-85
I just want to be Right 86
I'm Sorry 87
I Repent 88
In a time of need 89
Launch 90
Learn 91
Libra 92
Next 93
Prayer 94
Quick Thought 95
Quiet Time 96
Range 97
Restoration 98
Return 99
Sand, Breeze, and Rock 100
Simple Life 101
Spiritual Message on My Wrist 102
The Mind 103
The Struggle 104
There is Room 105
What do I do? 106
Wonderful 9:59am 107
Zenith 108
87 109

Horizon

Abundant Beauty from the Cross

I am wishing I could paint the cross on a canvas,
So I must paint the picture with these words
It takes time to analyze each sentence, each line
The reality is when I wear a cross on a necklace
My mind is focused in a new direction
People say that's a nice cross
You mean the diamonds I bought?
Are we not focused on the war HE fought,
So we can have the chance for eternal life?
The wooden cross carried down that road,
Harsh critics from the crowd,
Thrones from the crown
Now my diamonds gleam and sparkle
But the truth is the shine came through
Because darkness could not defeat the light
The coal trying to contain what is meant to be free
Now you can see the beauty of the cross
When the beautiful stone is released
The stone is removed from the tomb
And it shines so bright
When I wear the cross
I know the true beauty of it
It's called sacrifice

No greater love than a friend
That would lay down his life

Agape

God created us to create,
Our creation through God's guidance and grace,
nothing can replace the love I feel,
Husband and Wife created a child,
A precious gift,
Unconditional love sent from above,
A daughter in our mist,
The definition of true bliss,
Forever glowing from her first kiss,
I never felt love like this,
Thankful for this ultimate blessing,
Agape

Best Kind of Love

Best kind of love is forgiveness
Best kind of love is understanding
Best kind of love is caring
Best kind of love is pure
Best kind of love is the one that comes from God

The rock is my foundation
And the Dove for enhancement,
This is how I got to "Inspirations"
When Jesus says yes, nobody can say no

Connection

In life you have to be still like a mannequin
This way you can move
As God has intended you to move
Sometimes you have to pause
So the music can stop and collect your thoughts,
The silence of motion sitting on the sand,
Waves from the ocean, I stare in the great beyond,
the author of time speaks,
Number 6 is important to complete this series,
650 white on white you must give up,
Your precious gift is here,
Your foundation was set to be a great father,
Time to start the next chapter
With unconditional love, sent from above,
It's a victory, I thought I was whole,
Now I'm enhanced with a radiant glow,
The tears flow with joy,
Now I'm so bold,
The way the story is told,
I just want you to be proud of who I am,
I can't change my past,
The present is a gift and you are exactly my wish,
tomorrow I will prepare to hear His voice,
The inspiration is to find mediation

Deeper than what you see

The diamond cross pendant
The meaning more than you can see,
It's not about the why it gleams,
It's about the river streams
Through the lake of my dreams,
The baptism to make me clean,
Asking for forgiveness, repenting of my ways
That separate me from my calling,
That gentle reminder
That the light is always shining,
The Cross
Jesus protected me when I was lost,
The sacrifice that is a priceless cost,
The invitation to a better place,
Heaven my safe haven,
A mansion waiting on streets of gold,
But right now those stones sitting in gold,
I shall wear a crown when it's all over,
My savior has appointed me,
So no matter the struggle or obstacles,
I must remember the true meaning
Of the beauty of the cross,
How You love me so and never let me go,
When life was upside down,
YOU turned it all around,
Yes Jesus Loves me, the beauty of the cross
The symbolism of the Love for others...
Love someone today

Dosage of Praise

Lord speak to my heart,
Message of love to encourage me,
If I can hear from you then I'll know what to do,
We're blessed, it's going to work in your favor

I shall wear a crown, when it's all over

Enhancement

You enhance my life,
From the moment you were in my arms,
I knew I wanted to be everything
a father is supposed to be,
God guide me to be who I need to be,
And like the giving tree,
I want to share great things with you,
I want to give you everything in this world
to make you happy,
I want to teach you only joy comes from God,
This is critical for our foundation
As humans will disappoint you,
I pray I never disappoint you
And if I do I ask for you to forgive me
And continue to love me for
How God intended me to be,
Your smile and your laugh as pushed me
Through days you can't imagine,
I get sad I think how you will never
Know my brother, your uncle,
It's little things we want to control,
I pray to be there for you,
For each prized moment, that you cherish,
Just the other day you grab my finger
So I could walk with you,
You may think I'm guiding you
But in reality you are guiding me,
You are helping me to keep a clean heart,
To focus on the light and not the dark,
Also to give you all of my kisses

Enhancement continued

And to focus on all of my wishes,
Which is to love like my Savior...
Sacrifice so you can have the better life...
I love you more than you can imagine.

Expression

When I talked about inspirations
The reality is it came from my foundation
Through creation
It brought enhancement to my soul,
As I intricately put together each book
To reach where I'm at, or to explain my growth,
As I continue to be the mobile church,
The temple that dwells in me,
It's in my grasp it's in my reach,
I just have to remain focus on HIM,
I am his precious gem,
Yes Jesus loves me, my most important Hymn,
I still push on and maintain,
For HE is the only one who reigns,
I still experience sunshine and rain,
Joy and pain,
"Fly like a bird"
Still uplifts my spirits,
My soul is free
And the light flickers through the prism,
I refuse to be locked into the secular prison,
I'm going to execute the vision of my platform to
express HIS name,
I'm all about the spiritual,
The mind the pen the paper releasing new material,
my goal is to create enhance inspire,
And to take this higher...
As I walk with God

Foreign Land

Hard to be honored in your own house,
People not recognizing your whereabouts,
As I continue to evaluate,
Let's celebrate the Enhancement,
Not a street prophet, not evangelist,
I am an author at the altar,
Leaving my concerns with YOU ,
In the morning I'm renewed,
It's something about blue,
YOU bring me peace, the joy, the love,
I can relax and write my entries of
How YOU got me through,
YOU are my rock, I can't make it with YOU,
Your my foundation.
As I look at the infinity pool that almost
Connects to the ocean waves,
The beauty of man-made with your creation
Helps me understand
How we try to perfect ourselves
But we will never come close to your vast depth,
So I trust in YOU
Because I know you order my steps,
I relax and enjoy the breeze,
Joy in my heart and my mind at ease,
YOU bring me peace

Infinity pool watching my wife hold my daughter
I open up my journal,
Another passage from this author

Gala

Create the great escape in my mind I can't wait,
Dreaming today because it's never too late
Step by step, pace by pace,
Give me a little space on this race,
Victory I embrace,
The Art Gallery displays the face,
The face of faith, asking for this in advance,
So when it's time to land,
People will understand
This was written in my journal,
This was a part of my plan, let's dance,
Music for a gala let's give to charity,
A billion smiles, one smile at a time,
Time after time let's accomplish what we seek,
discover the art of giving, speak then repeat,
praying to put these admirations in reach

Give

20 years has passed…
I'm still trying to adjust to a new method,
Priorities of giving first, lifestyle last,
So I can extend more help, more assistance,
I want to give like a mission,
Time, talent and resources,
I want to make the practical choices,
I want to limit the designer wear,
Eliminate the status of being in the know,
Eliminate the perception of that's all a show,
I want to focus on growth of helping others,
Doing charity, celebrating community outreach,
Being a blessing, show I'm a human that's kind,
All of this done in silence without promotion,
No earthly praise, my reward in heaven…

Matthew 6: 3-4

God made me

God made me
Mo City raised me
Houston amazed me
Jesus saved me

If life is a movie
Then the Afterlife is the sequel
Job well done, the golden gates are open for you,
A mansion set aside because you were true,
True to your heart

Mama's teachings brought my passion
She was the one that brought these books to action,
My dad's desire was to get a car with a horse,
So when I needed a new car
I looked at the symbol on the Porsche
Lights, camera, every person is a star
Build a foundation this is how you get this far
Really it's God's Grace, he shows the picture,
I grabbed the pencil and begin to trace,
Sometimes I colored outside the lines,
I'm human I'm not divine,
He said keep coloring everything is fine,
You have freedom of choice
Even though you are my design,
And in due time I came back to HIS intentions,
Look at His artwork

Heart

No matter the situation....
Speak to my heart...
Cleanse my heart, fill it with abundant love,
Let my heart display your fruits and goodness...
Lord, I need you now more than ever...
The time is now, to do your works,
YOU are my rock and treasure,
Let me use my gifts and talents
that you have given me in a way
that displays your power and glory.
Lord, guide me on your path & show me your way.
Let my heart continue to grow,
Continue to illuminate
My path for a successful journey.

Proverbs 3:5-8
Psalms 51:10

Highest of all time

As my spirit continues to grow
And my thoughts soar through the clouds
My desires are lifted off the ground
The music plays a beautiful sound

Love is Easy

I want to love easy,
I want to erase the pain in my heart,
I want to love like God, the love that's easy,
Only forgiveness
and opportunities for improvement,
I don't want to make it hard,
I want love easy but I keep looking at my scar,
So I look to God and Jesus shows me HIS' scars,
So I know Love is easy, see where I been,
That's how I made it this far, in the darkness,
HE appeared "the shining star",
So I ask that I love easy,
I ask You to erase all of my doubts,
eliminate my judgements
like I have been better than my counterparts
Because You know I was the one making it hard.
Lord, cleanse my heart,
Let me love easy like You,
Today is my new start
Let me love unconditional
Agape

No Ceiling

When I'm with you,
You don't understand what unconditionally means,
however you demonstrate it
Whenever you are with me
You are my baby forever,
This feeling lets me love you differently
There is no ceiling for what I would do for you,
This feeling is so beyond,
Where it touches the heavens
And comes back to protect you,
The electricity, the thunder, the lighting,
That power that is from beyond,
All I can tell you is that it's the best feeling,
It carries me through the day,
I would give you the world if I could,
My life, my purpose is to raise you right,
Show you love,
So you understand that love
Heals, reveals and conquers all,
There is no ceiling,
I'm just showing how God intended love,
There is no limit with you,
Genuine Love

Out of Darkness

One of the most critical things
You need in this world is a foundation.
The early teachings I received
was a model for the period of darkness in my life.
Those routines of going to church every Sunday
were implanted into my mindset
when I was young.
My mother took my brother and I
to church every day of our lives until we were 18.
As I got older I knew that the church
was just a building not the temple.
The temple is inside of me.
Jesus is living inside of me.
I am a mobile temple that goes to a church building
for treatment or to encourage others.
As I continue to enhance my thinking,
I know my books serve as a beacon to reach people
with the purpose of sharing the GOOD News.
The good news is Christ saves and renews,
HE is the light in the dark.
When you go through periods of darkness,
Please pursue HIM.
I have had a lot of dark moments in my life
And HE has brought me through…

Pray to God

I remember those nights when I felt alone
The battle against darkness and depression
The age of being exposed of the dangers of
not knowing the envy & plots of harm from others
I continue to pray to God for protection against evil.
I pray for kindness and
To display love to all I encounter,
To show bountiful wisdom of care,
And to continue to share HIS principles
To make this world a better place,
As I focus on the mission of being
A fisherman of men,
I pray that I share HIS word
And to be encouragement for that soul
That needs to be saved,
These tears are real when we come back to HIM,
I pray we dive into these open arms....
Thank you Jesus

Seeds

My purpose,
My test,
The testimony
I went through and going through
Is to get closer to God
"My discovery of God
And how it has brought me through life
And my foundation for everything going forward,
If it involves the "Messiah First",
Then I will sign off on it."
The MF signature

Stone

As I reflect...
I wish I could take his pain away,
I keep telling myself,
This is something I can't change
There is no one to blame;
It is hard to change pain
I know he loved you dear,
And as his sibling the truth is from the beginning
I try to steer him away from you...
In another direction,
I try to let him see my perspective
But what I learned is a true blessing;
Love can keep people together,
Love can define the odds,
No matter the cause or the obstacle
Love never lets go
He remained true but it was you
Who opened up my books and you knew
You read, you told him how much
He is in my heart
Since the times we were young
You understood, I'm thanking you later
Because I didn't at the time
I love my nephews, I see you in them
As I rewind, in my pages you will live forever
Charlie's Angel
....
Tieashia Jones Ford

Supportive

You were more than supportive
You were my number one fan
You would come to the games
And I knew no matter the outcome
You would be by my side, Time after time
When I was in trouble
You were there to guide me through,
As time grew being supportive
The example was you,
A bond that still holds,
The rock that never folds,
Even today, I still feel your support,
You saying you can do it, believe in those plans,
People will buy your product,
Gain a small following....
You were definitely supportive,
I miss you Brother

Strings in my Heart

You fixed the strings in my heart,
Your mother was the start
You took the rest and completed the light
When I was in the dark
You're my shining star,
Here and far, you have no idea,
How you erased the pain in my heart,
You have erased the pain
Of me missing your uncle by far,
You will never know him
But you have to understand
He loved me from my start
On days you look at the frames
With the babies playing their part,
The Lord knew you was the part,
To help heal my heart because when I'm with you,
I know how I got this far…love,
Which is the answer from the start
His Grace and mercy,
What is complicated and hard is so easy,
So continue, to smile
And erase your Daddy's pain through the seasons,
Christ is the reason,
Help me as I have committed treason
Of being uneasy of the loss,
You will never know,
But God allowed you to fix the strings in my heart,
your love is easy
And you have helped ease me from the start,
9/6/17 to now,
Love you always, the strings in my heart

The Natural Number following 5 & preceding 7

When I wake up, I think of you
When I pray, I think of you
When I reflect, I think of you
When I am creating, I think of you,
When I am enhancing I think of you
When I am inspiring, I think of you

Six times around my mind and I am back to you
Daddy loves you
And I am so grateful for the blessing you are

The Spirit of Sam/Sam Made me Smile

As I sat there and I listened to the stories
I tried to focus only on the glory
Each word little by little
Brought me to a different place
It has been a while since I saw the young boy
Where I remembered his face
He was such a vibrant and cool kid with that charm
As I move along, he was 29 and now he is gone
My mind is in a different space
But I'm in a familiar place
A place where my neighbors love me
As they loved themselves
I received so much love
Those Daily Breads was placed in my hands
Those prayers in the car before school on demand
The Williams family
I would not have made it without you
The sacrifice and the care
As I looked at the program, I stared
I heard the how come and the what if
I listened to the poem to his father and mother,
What a gift, it brings tears to my eyes,
I listened to Isaiah say no one truly dies
The spirit of Sam is alive
He lives in our hearts
Isaiah 57:1, protection from what was to come
I look back at the pictures for a while; I see the style
I time traveled, I covered miles,
You brought me back to the days with Granny
Sam, you made me smile

Three

The author
The poet
The speaker

Like a chemist, mix them together in a beaker,
I'm a kingdom seeker, 3 styles one feature
My human nature,
If they ask why, that's just the way it is,
Lord, grant me the words
And wisdom to deliver only Your intentions,
The flickering light in this prism,
Let the world see the radiant colors you produce,
I must stay connected to Vine to produce the fruit,
continue to garden my ways,
And for me to display I have been saved,
If it wasn't for your grace,
then I couldn't use this pen to trace the blessings
you have provided, continue to speak to my heart,
Father, Son and Holy Spirit...three

Truth

The truth is I could never let you go
The truth is I could never leave you
The truth is I couldn't do that to you
The truth is I could spend a lifetime with you
The truth is I would be lost without you
The truth is I would give the world to you
The truth is I love you differently
The truth is it's called unconditionally

Velocity

Just to be close to You,
Every Word is true,
It's your path I pursue,
I choose to honor You and grow each day,
What more can I say ,
Each day I'm renewed,
Thank you for Your Grace and Mercy,
So many times I have fallen short of your Glory,
The many shortcomings,
Trapped in this world's pleasures,
Give me the strength to resist those desires,
And through the fire, Your hand is there,
Give me the strength to pull forward
And conquer where it pleases You

Velocity

Wonderful Change

A wonderful change has come over me
As I reminisce on how it used to be
The dark nights, life in the streets,
A wonderful change has come over me
A renewal of HIS commandments,
Love God with all your heart
This is how I started
To make the improvement in my life
And what a wonderful change
That has come over me
Guided to the light,
Open my eyes what a beautiful sight
A wonderful change has come over me

Innovation

Abandonment

So this is what I thought,
And what I wrote in my mind at the time
It was quiet, I put everything in place
I thought once, I thought twice,
Is this what I want to do?
She was at work, I neatly packed my bags
I picked up the phone and called a cab
I left without a trace, I left the door unlock
I left with no note, letter, or card, no reason
No please disregard me being so rude
The night before I held you so close
And stared at the moon,
Looking at the city lights, all these thoughts came
So I wrote them down put them in a bottle
I didn't put the bottle where it could be found
I simply threw it in the trash
I made sure no was around
Had I took my steps back,
Really forward to my next encounter
I wonder, I ponder,
What is the meaning of being selfish?
What is the meaning of together?
The meaning of us, the meaning of we,
The meaning of me?
So I decide to search the globe for the answer,
The uncertainties, and the unknown
I left because I decided to search for home
But I stayed
Because I thought I could make a difference
And I believed in us
The Courage of Commitment

Allure

From the day I saw that charisma of
have fun until the funds become limited,
which never happen,
from the time when I meet you,
you just got the new ES 300,
I was young college student,
you were all about mathematics,
with a biology and chemistry degree,
Here's the equation you gave to me,
The formula is commerce,
Which makes the world go round,
When I'm on Beverly Hill I don't make sound,
The reflection it's all about those Italian drivers,
Lunch at Magnolia Bar and Grill,
The Diver Scallops, crab fingers, gumbo and salad,
The simple Cartier Pasha watch,
Nothing made me feel flyer,
than riding in the pumpkin spice Hummer,
listening to Erykah Badu all summer,
in the backseat Beautiful call me littleboydrummer,
I'm passing that Old Farm, from dusk to dawn,
My college years, this is where I belong,
I'm in memory lane, as I bring you along,
It's a part of the process of healing,
The sky is the limit,
It's the ceiling that we can't see,
I'm back at Memorial Oaks,
How can this be?
This can't be life?
It was all good last night...

Allure continued

Then the morning came,
A new direction let me be precise,
You are still Mr. Nice,
The influence to these designers' brands,
The definition of showing love,
Gone but not forgotten,
I look above, and the dove gives me hope,
The allure as I flashback
To Ford F150 the window is down,
I feel the breeze from the weather,
We are late to the airport
You are overly excited singing Lucky Star
Seating on King Ranch Leather,
That smile of yours always made things better,
As I try to keep it together,
Sometimes it gets harder
Then I laugh and say they see that red stripe,
That's Prada

Back in the starting blocks

As I knell, squat, I'm back in the starting blocks,
I'm ready to run and get my sprint on
I gave all of my efforts,
I treated you as I would treat myself,
Comfortable living,
What do you need?
Why did I return?
The good life of a great writing time?
767 fly on to the destination,
TV screens in the headrest
As I get older, these times never felt so well,
What I thought was a boulder...
Really was a small stepping-stone for life,
I will conquer my pride
Back in Houston working on my new book
Indmix snapping pictures,
A'bouzy supports my addiction,
My necklace glisten, jewelry by *King Johnny*,
There is your free marketing,
See I mention you in a sentence,
Laughing out loud
One day the 7 books will be finally finished,
New accomplishments coming soon
7/31/2020

Basic

Short and precise
Keep it simple and keep it nice
No hidden meanings, just keep it direct
No variety, no restaurant flight of beverages
Just a simple entree,
That's who people are trying to make me be...
However, I'm not born that way
Sorry...
I'm a thinker, creator and enhancer

Check

If I'm lost like a penny with a hole in it
But my display is smooth
Earth, Wind and Fire,
Its darkness but I'm in the groove
What should I expect?
No one can see the pain, I think?
Did I push the button to make sure it would sync?
My mind too great to fix this question,
The series of them
No more trips to the past or the quest for the future
What does or where does this leave me?
A man caught up in his work, I am in the office,
Checking times, operating pages of mine
Thinking of new riddles, new rhymes,
Listening to music
It's Bigger than my body
Something's missing,
I understand that line

Beverage... check....
Food... check...
Clothes... check...

Google

As I sip my glass of water
Maybe nothing is missing at all
Trust the scripture

Matthew 6:25

Dish

I remember being young,
I like to cook and make dishes
I see at the fancy restaurants.
I didn't care about what my friends
Thought about my hobby.
They eventually love to come over
and sample some item I came up with.
I believe there is no rules to imagination.
No different in the kitchen.

So I would switch our ingredients all the time.

Who says I can't make King's Stew?

King's Stew is like gumbo
But with ingredients I wanted to put in it:
King Crab Meat
(Already removed from the shell),
Colossal scallops,
Jumbo prawns,
Oysters,
Wild boar sausage,
Quail meat...

Factory Rest

Monday
Tuesday
Wednesday
Thursday
Friday
Saturday
Sunday
Instagram, Twitter, Facebook, Snapchat
I'm think I'm covered for information
However my storage needs to be managed
Cars, Clothes, Jewelry, Food Blogging my delights
Something about this doesn't seem right
Too much secular world,
I want to get back to the simple life
Exercise, pray, and relax
I need a factory reset
Which simply means just focus more on God

Fallback

As I fallback to putting pen to paper,
Early in the morning,
What should be the topic to savor,
As I reflect, my struggle is the sip and savor,
Time for a detox, a cleanse of my life,
I have thought about it once
I have thought about it twice,
As I try to channel my introvert-ness,
I continue to get emails that make me a socialite,
I must be out to sale these books,
So people see who I am
Like Prince "You got the look,
I rather sit at home and cook,
I enjoy these 5am times in my journal,
Quiet time to express my thoughts,
Time change fallback its extra dark,
Detox, paper to pen again is a good start,
A small flame of thoughts ready to spark,
One of my goals is to express this art,
Fallback a renaissance man,
Sunday tunes will be Jazz,
I'll put on the brown robe to be like my dad,
I love you more today than yesterday
But not as much as tomorrow that's Happy Talk,
Fallback one hour back,
Pen to paper, you are back, so I smile

Free Living

I'm going 0-60,
Now I'm on the toll way…70, 80, 90,100
I'm free living
I'm thinking of the beginning, my life as a child
Thinking of my up bringing,
Church doors kick open
The choir is singing,
Late night walking to the park shooting baskets
My escape from the madness,
It's tragic, it's reality, not magic
The way the tears build a small pond
As I move along,
I'm reaching, now I'm in the present
My foot on the pedal all the way down;
I'm at 117 need to slow it down;
I just wanted to make the old man proud
Now I'm just free living,
I'm reading Matthew
And I know my riches won't get me to heaven
But my faith will
I'm just free living; I'm giving pieces of my heart
I'm praying that's my spark
Teardrops flow quietly from my eye;
I'm mentally drained
But it doesn't stop my thoughts, read my thoughts
My intentions is to bring peace and love
Only joyful vibes will erase
My mind's pain of us not being together

Karma

She's in love with an image, not me
They say the apple don't fall too far from the tree
But I'm God's seed like mustard
Faith
But she doesn't trust it
She just wants apples for the custard
Something sweet, overlooking reality
The beauty in me, the rings of growth
The bark will show, the pain and depression like
Edgar Allen Poe
The Pendulum, the blade cutting me nice and slow
…A shadow
I ponder I realize this
You have shared my world;
You have been next to my girl
Her voice fades from the phone; it's diminished
We are finished; it can't be rekindled
Fading pictures of us in my mind
But it's a shadow behind us in the frames
I was so glad you came; now we are distant
It has ended
My thoughts of a reconnection
Years later, now I understand the shadow existence
Let me put it in perspective
Karma, you a trip, you taught me a lesson

Looking Back on Vanity

I'm in love with the better half of me,
The rich black lustrous goatee with the smooth skin
The charm, the hustle to make things happen
What happen, sacrifices made
Some called it maturity, some called it change
I'm losing my ability to see those days
Those personal accomplishments
Mostly faded pictures showing my ego
The younger me, being tested by faith
That drive that me marketable,
That goal of more gold more money to fold
Life of the young and restless, Life of the Bold
…and the Beautiful
The days were I felt I was the chosen one
Embracing the gift and the curse,
Everybody wants to be a star
Days of our lives, One Life to Live
Trying to build a Dynasty
The other half of me said look at the Guiding Light
Another world and as the world turns
Now I focus on Matthew 6:33 instead of vanity

Man with the Beard

On days I reflect on that beard
That brought me tears,
Some of the pain
Some of the joy
The deep voice that made me believe I was trouble
That coarse hair that stubble when I was a boy
Now that I'm a man
I find myself growing a beard to connect you,
As look in the mirror
I wonder when we were children, my brother and I
I look to the sky, those were the times,
Now it's time to fly
I have my own reasons for that growth,
Sometimes it's being lazy
Or
The ego driven words that you favor Marvin Gaye,
I'm wearing the red skull hat, a Motown special,
A continual blessing,
I start to wonder about this awesome gene,
It's called bloodline, thank you Pops

My Packed Bag (Quondam Contemplation)

As I turn the pages of months after months
As I write without the passion of desire,
I must explain
YOU were everything I needed and more
YOU penetrated my heart's inner core
YOU opened up that door
One long journey of the life I dreamed,
Spending evenings on laughs and a good time
I shouldn't rewind those precious minutes and hours
I should balance to make this right
Because every book, every poem, every night,
Every weekend, every evening
That ability to reflect on an experience
Makes this life out of sight
These memories are what completes me,
Makes these moments what they are,
A pure treasure, a ruler of life,
This is how I measure obstacles, milestones…
My bag is packed with the necessary accessories;
the reflection of a smile
I am ready for more of the adventure of mine….
As YOU as my guide?
Philippians 4:4
five, six, seven, eight, and nine

Over Dose

Too many features,
Too many chemicals in the beaker
premium goods...I'm buying too many sneakers
Too many Tees, Too many Jeans, Too many Teas
A lot of herbs, a lot of spices
A lot of vices, too many devices
Like Hollywood the pressure running
Through the veins, seeing white lines — - - ——
I'm overdosing because I'm having a good time
Too many dreams, not enough sleep
Too many pills a week, passing the daily dosage
Too much consumption
Promethazine codeine mixed with Sprite
Good times...I'm headed to the light
Overdose...my body putting up a fight
I'm overdosing because I'm living the life
Too many good times, too many awesome options
Overdose! I can't stop it!
Now, I'm over the dose
....
Maybe we should be overdosing on Jesus

Perceptions and Illusions

On new days, I want to explore
But I'm trapped in the great indoors,
So on days I want to explore,
The Internet is whom I adore
She takes me from store to store; we shop
And in a few days at the house, boxes will stop.
Move, refresh, and click…what's new in stock?
Can I get back from this quarter life crisis?
New gadgets, new devices, and new meals
I will try with different spices,
Maybe, all I am good at is writing,
Better yet writing to myself,
I took a risk when I wrote my SOS to the world,
I thought it was creative
The way the two stories were told…through one,
The lines of the author
Explaining before and after through rhymes,
Maybe I'm trapped inside
Because there are no more signs…of adventure,
Did I fail to mention,
I'm exploring through potential,

It's not complete
I'm a project waiting to perfect
Each passage, each sentence, each story
I live through grace and I dance in glory,
No one sees these feelings
Because I'm trapped inside but I'm looking out,
Help me… I'm in recovery…time to rediscover.

Prescription

Drink Plenty of Water
Read Daily Bible Verse twice in the morning
Listen to the OnePlace App: The Alternative
Read Daily Bible Verse twice in the evening
Drink Plenty of Water

Searching for a Signal

Repentance, confessions, valuable lessons
I need a signal to get a clear picture of the vision
Hashtags and mentions,
Distractions of true intentions,
Lord,
Clear the air waves so the clarity is crystal clear,
The good news is what I want to hear,
Geneva Sound Lab play music softly,
Christian and Gospel another way to be connected,
Yes, Jesus loves me, I feel so special,
The beauty of the cross displayed on my necklace,
the white in the clouds, the blue sky,
His thoughts aren't our thoughts,
HE reveals now
I'm slowly understanding, it's joy for the journey.
Divine reason rescue me from spiritual treason

September Rest

I had a dream that Tupac said
"I like your style, you could be more political
But I dig the fact you're more spiritual,
I like that you're smooth and lyrical,
Your message is different"
I said, "I like yours because you were militia
You let your words bleed, the pain in your voice
Let them feel those emotions,
You gave subjects, and left those wide open.
You were THUG LIFE and important,
You bridge the gap for knowledge,
the census, and the reports
You definitely reached
You sold 67 millions records worldwide
"Who can compete?"
He said, "Keep doing what you are doing"
I said, "How did you do it"
He said
"O…. I see…that was the easy part
I just believed in me, you're on the right path,
you believe that you're the poet in the tree."

Research John Holyfield "the poet"

Spike Lee's New Actor

As I direct this entry like a director directs a movie
I look for something to move me
Like the people in Brooklyn
They seem to be viewed as the great ones
Like Jordan dropping fifty, points that is
Or Biggie dropping dope lines,
That transfer to hot rhymes
Or maybe it's just a New York thing,
As I direct the scene,
The screen is moving around the scene,
The person I mean, the actor is still
Still the background moves along the reel
Its touch is so magical, inspired by Spike Lee
Here's your new actor
What I act is factual
Real life, real words, real nouns, real verbs
It's golden; silence the curtains are pulling,
Silence is golden
Here's my blurb

"Keep Dreaming"

The Path to Normality

No time to argue or debate
Idle thoughts, no more questions,
Leads to limited expression of who I am
A part of my heart is **damaged**
And I think it can't be repaired
I don't know the answers;
But I am allowed to ask the questions
My feelings need to be transferred back to reality
The only true question is…
…is this best for me?
…My thoughts of wants and needs have been
activated back to normality
What is the meaning of being selfish?
Why seek fairness?
Time for my simple response…
Okay

Tranquility

Take me to another zone
"Where you are not alone',
There is 'no hole in my soul",
"My mind is my home"
As I embrace the wind,
The words come with such ease
Laughing out loud did
"Someone move my Cheese?"
A book I need to read
As I sit here looking at the nature of the present
Palm trees, speculator weather
As I take a deep breath, I get it all together
Magical thoughts
"Wherever there is good, it can only get better"
Immaculate structure of words being delivered
...from my thoughts
An intoxicating view brings a "new" translation:
True words from the heart
One small spark can create a great flame;
A great flame was created by a little spark
My thoughts still remain extraordinary,
"Extra" ordinary,
Even through delightful frustrations
The world moving at my speed, perfect rotation
As I search the globe for world destinations,
"Where else should we go?"

As my mind departures from the homeland,
As I consume, Peaceful thoughts on Earth
Waiting on a vacation

Vote

Valuable
Opportunity
To
Excel

Wait for Me

Time and patience are hard to gauge
So go with your heart
but let your mind guide your heart's thoughts
I say, "Let your mind control your emotions"
I guess, I will make the same good choice again,
which is;
What they are calling a mistake.
They say "Go with your feelings"; if that is the case
Baby, please wait for me to follow my _____
I apologize for the wrong choice,
Which was following my ____

The blanks are to be filled in with the words "heart, mind or mind, heart". Whichever one fits your situation place them where they belong.

War of Women

As I approach the door, I realize
I must step back, I must ask
Which one of you belongs in my past?
I'm at the core of my life
Is it you I enjoy waking up to the nature's breeze?
Is it you who knows me best
And enjoys my company?
Is it you who reads my words
When I send you the manuscript?
Is it you who reads my book,
The one that smiles and gives me that look?
As I approach the door, I realize
I must elevate, I must stay on task
Which one of you belongs in my present?
Your kind heart makes me remember your presence
Your sweet words create a natural essence
I'm at the core of this lesson;
My answer needs to be precise
Out of sight but in my mind,
I just want to get it right
As I take a walk in the sunlight,
It feels good being who I am
Not a new kid on the block but "I'll be loving you"
till there is none left,
Do I choose the right or the left?
Or the center of attention,
I like these discussions on the staircase
or in the kitchen
Which one of you belongs in my future?
I simply answer by closing my eyes
as I put on my headphones & listen to the music

Winter Breeze

California Dreaming is how
I discovered Zion Riots Wear, Venice Beach,
It's something about LA, never thought
Bob Marley shirts would get me paid,
Now I'm relaxing Otis Redding,
Sitting at the dock of the bay,
Time to walk on by like Issac Hayes,
When I received that first payment
It was Happy Feelings
Like Frankie Beverly and Maze,
I'm amazed even today that I saw the wave
As I looked at the waves,
As the time moves away I decided to change lanes,
premium goods shoe wear,
Couriering exclusives in advance,
I took that chance,
That's how I won the contest in the 2nd grade
When I decided to dance,
I went with "that" feeling this may work,
Like Bobby Womack said it's a winter's day
So I stopped into church,
A reflection in my heart, the temple is there
reminding me of my start,
Got on my knees and begin to pray...
5:45 a.m. the alarm goes off Aretha Franklin
Featuring Mavis Staples "O Happy Day",
Quick notes and I'm on my way...
California Dreaming

Young Man

I was once like you,
I made it through the different stages,
Read about my life through these pages
I share to help you, elevate you,
We all don't make it I can see every,
Moment that I was lost
And saved through those mistakes,
No guarantee I was going to make it
If I had to do it again the same way,
I know I wouldn't make it,
That's why I say eliminate the distractions
And focus on God, seek Him, that's the safe haven,
the kingdom is there for you,
Take the path He's illuminating, Be Bold
The struggles I've been through,
I once was like you, He saved me,
Seek the Light and the Truth

111.11

I purpose in my heart the gift from the start,
Out of love the five ones from above,
The ones equal five, the number of grace,
As continue with my five senses
Which helps me execute
What is being heard and taught,
I think deep a lot...this is a grace gift,
Which is my spirit saying this is goodness and favor from God.
No hesitation, no compulsion, happy to provide....the number five

2, 4, 5 and 6

Love, Grace & Imani is my introduction
Discovering Devotion is the masterpiece
Inspirations from God is my direction
Foundation is my connection
2, 4, 5 and 6

2005

2016

2018

2019

Structure

ABillionsmiles

It's more than you and it's more than me
So let's encourage others to take the stand
And share that smile and every once in a while
they'll see we are there,
Step by step, day by day
We will grow this energy of care,
We can go anywhere one smile at a time

Use your courage to make others Smile

Today's goal
Do one nice random act of kindness

One of these things
-Buy a stranger's lunch
-Buy a stranger's groceries in line
-Give an encouragement card with a gift card

#couragecauses
#abillionsmiles

Once I accomplish this goal,
The next goal is to do it each day...
Something random and nice
That will make someone SMILE

Thank you for a seat at the table
So I can help others
Thank you that I can listen and learn from others

Acknowledgement

Through meditation and dedication
Of being the person I desire,
I shield off those desires that make me lose focus,
there is no magic wand or potion,
It's just prayer to God to clean me of things
That prevent me from being the best I can,
It's not by luck or chance
That I survived those storms,
It was the wind that helped me
Gain balance on the mountain,
It was the seeds deposited in me
Before I flipped a coin into the fountain,
Still dreaming my dreams
And executing the visions placed before me,
Thankful for those who believe in the process
Of praying for me to achieve
Becoming a better individual each day,
You are appreciated

Fingerprints

When I trace the design to the paper,
I hope it reflects I'm a child of God,
I know I have shaded outside the lines,
Let me repent,
I want to live up to my calling of being heaven sent,
let my sins be rinse,
My concentration on drawing
Is becoming more intense,
I want the light to shine as it's supposed to,
Illuminate my fingerprints to show my growth,
Let my roots continue to expand,
Let me be able to show my hands of gratitude,
Let me spread your Word latitude and longitude
across the globe by the way of writing
As I use my fingerprint to open my iPhone,
Typing entries in notes,
Thank you for the Grace, Love and Hope,
Same message, a different approach…

Fraction

As I walk on the beach
And the Music says "Until hurt YOU"
As the music bring the tears to my face
As I sit in my heart's church pews,
I reminisce on how I lost a few,
The few I still yearn to hear their words again,
Only if the iPhone had
Recorded the moments I'm looking for,
I thought my foolish pride was enough
However it falls short, one of my fears
Is that I forget to think about you daily,
Depression comes and goes lately,
I feel that I'm changing,
I'm searching for the ones
that were there in the beginning,
denying the fact that I can't speak to you,
I still have visions of you
Coming in that blue hue of glow,
I know you, I see you so clear,
The only thing is I know that love keeps me close,
I can't hide the fact what you meant to me,
From the day you first hurt me,
Until now that I'm still hurting
That this chapter has ended,
I never thought how long it would be
But I see it's not as long as I wanted,
I thought I knew what to do
when I would be without you, but that's not true,
few I trust, few of them I actually communicate,
through time I realize I couldn't hide,

Fraction continued

I looked in the mirror and realize I hurt you,
So what do I do, I must embrace this book,
The foundation has already been set,
Give more to foundations to offset,
The pain, donating actually brings comfort
And therapy to help others,
I have faith that "it" will never go away
But it will ease the pain of missing you...
You didn't quit, you just knew when to walk away,
and I know you are smiling back at me...
I see you, your love is still here

Help

This is more than quiet time,
This is the time where I can reflect
On what I'm called to do,
How to execute plans,
This is my journal to keep me on the path,
The path of being righteous,
The path where I will ask for forgiveness,
the time to think if my body was locked in a prison,
the time where the light shines through the prism
and shows me the direction to go with the rays of
light, the beam that points to the dream ,
The dream of helping others, my only alternative
when I myself feel trouble,
Sometimes I suffer from depression,
Then I look around and see the blessings,
I remember to stay close for enhancement,
enhancement from the WORD,
And how HE has conquered the World
And I can do all things through Christ that
strengthens me, I was once blind but now I see,
HE has delivered me from my own understanding,
this planet is not our home,
We are just here to complete our mission,
Then it's to the Heavens
Where there are many mansions, streets of gold,
So I focus on becoming as you made me to be,
That breathe of air, that tree of life,
My only focus is to live right,
To fulfill God's Dream,
Us displaying love to each other…
Help someone

Help continued

Philippians 3:17-21 New American Standard Bible

17. Brethren, join in following my example, and observe those who walk according to the pattern you have in us. 18. For many walk, of whom I often told you, and now tell you even weeping, that they are enemies of the cross of Christ, 19. Whose end is destruction, whose god is their appetite, and whose glory is in their shame, who set their minds on earthly things. 20. For our citizenship is in heaven, from which also we eagerly wait for a Savior, the Lord Jesus Christ; 21. who will transform [n]the body of our humble state into conformity with the body of His glory, by the exertion of the power that He has even to subject all things to Himself.

I just want to be right

I want to be right
Look to the God for the fight
I want to be right
Keep me toward the light
I want to be right
The lion and lamb handle all of my plights
I want to be right
Lord restore my might
I want to be right in your sight

I'm Sorry

I'm sorry for being selfish
I'm sorry for moving on
I'm sorry for taking too long
I'm sorry for not helping out
I'm sorry for not empowering others
I'm sorry for my bad habits
I'm sorry for knowing what I want
I'm sorry for not expressing my thoughts
I'm sorry for bad decisions and my faults
I'm sorry that I don't understand
I'm sorry for not being there
I'm sorry that it looks like I don't care
I'm sorry for my passion
I'm sorry for asking
I'm sorry for my pride
I'm sorry for my wants and lifestyle
I'm sorry that it has nothing to do with me
I'm sorry that I can't help more

I Repent

I repent, I know YOU were heaven sent
Too many earthly distractions I'm constantly bent
Where has time went
I wasted time sometimes being foolish,
Sometimes being content
I repent
I need to give up some of my lifestyle
For a longer time than lent
I need to let those things go no matter my intent
I repent
I need to live more like You, and forgive
And display love
I need to repent for all those people I judged
I need to let go of all the baggage and the grudge
I repent for not seeing how I should live
Forgive me

In a time of need

As I hold God's hand through my pain and hurt
Slowly HE heals me,
Another one of HIS great works,
The molding and shaping of what I need
Lord take care of me
As I'm in the darkness like an onyx,
Restore me softly like you have done before,
Give me the faith
That there is nothing you won't and cannot do,
Let me accept your steps,
I know I fall short of glory,
You know all my excuses and sad stories,
Through it all remain here in my time of need,
Just like before when I was hungry,
You did feed, when I was dying of thirst,
You did bleed,
Lord help me achieve,
The greatness you have planned for me

Launch

When no one else believed I kept dreaming,
I kept pushing I kept searching for the answers
To bring me the clarity that achievement
was a reality for me in the areas I desired,
I made it through the fire of doubts,
Here I stand, seek the kingdom first
And it will be added

Learn

It took some time to realize that
There is no one I dislike,
Life is simple,
We do not like people's ways.
If a person changes their ways
Then you have no problem with them.
It's that simple...
So I pray that my ways that
Make me an unlikeable person are taken away.
I'm speaking of the ways that
Do not reflect I am a child of the kingdom.
So let me concentrate on treating others
With love at all time.

Libra

As I try to balance life
I think once, I think twice
I think day, I think night
Some days I get angry,
Some days I just smile
It's been sometime
Since I heard your voice in reality
I wish I could have archived our talks
The lessons I learned
The trials and tribulations that are testing me
I stay strong for others and mask the depression
As I look at pictures when we were young
I find the picture of you holding your son
How twenty years has passed
They say the days are slow and the years are fast
Some days are good, some days are sad
The memories that God supplied me I'm so glad
As I mentally tip the scales
To concentrate on the light and not the darkness
"The Light shines in the darkness, and
The darkness did not comprehend it." (John 1:5)
I know everything will be alright, October is here
22 reasons to celebrate

Next

As I drive early in the morning,
I turn the radio off to meditate in silence,
I ask myself why do I write books,
Is this my calling, is this what I'm meant to do?
Should I just keep it simple and just teach,
No publications from me...
I can just use this formula go to work,
Family time and plan trips.
I sometimes wonder how this all started?
Is this my way of drawing art through these words?
I could transition into a food blogger
Or what else could I do?
This is what I have done all my life,
Whether in a journal or a notepad.
This is how I clear my thoughts,
Decisions need to be made,
Contemplation

Prayer

Lord, my prayer is to protect my family, eliminate negative thoughts, to focus on the gifts in front of us...I'm human and I remember those experiences of the testing of faith, my main concern is to always keep my daughter safe, for her mother and me to be able to see what every parent wants, the cycle of life, those stages and to be there when she crosses those stages, praying for Your Grace and Mercy...

In Jesus name, Amen

Quick Thought

As I search through my foundation
Sometimes my struggle is I think of yesterday
And live for the moment at hand
I force myself to think of tomorrow
What am I to learn from my past?
I know you can fight or flight
Most of the times I choose to remain out of sight
I silently gather my might

Quiet Time

The creation of stillness
As my mind is listening to the instruction of God,
HE tells me to focus on what HE has for me,
In that moment I know the direction
That is intended for me...
I see the scripture's meaning...
I know HE will battle my enemies,
Which in some cases are myself against myself,
Give me the strength to pursue your message
Of becoming what you intended me to be, a disciple

Range

I silently think about my diverse background,
The key is to have a firm foundation
That allows you to value things that are different
But doesn't change who you are
And what you believe.
There are so many people
We can learn great information from,
However, we let little things block our ability
To gather what is being attempted to be delivered.
One of the fundamental components in belief is
to be confident in what you like and desire.
Be bold and go after what you want.
This is how I aspired for cultural learning & travel.

Restoration

As I look for reinstatement
From the following situation
I was like the prodigal son,
I had left for a good time,
The grass is greener on the other side
Or maybe I was more like Lot in lands
Some where I didn't belong,
I'm thankful to God he has brought me home,
My soul has been restored
I'm back to my original design,
Factory settings back to normal,
God order my steps
Now use me for the vessel I am meant to be
...moving forward

Return

Through years of progression,
I think about life's lessons,
The joy and the pain,
I'm focusing of the blessing of
How I made it this far,
The foundation set when I was young,
Later I would become dependent
On those truths to get me through,
To be honest I need them day by day,
Give me the peace to surpass my mistakes
And open my arms for that embrace.
Lord I'm coming back to you

Sand, Breeze and Rock

Now I travel to clear water to keep my soul clean
My mind is free from the world,
It's the breeze that I embrace,
Love patterns I trace to display God's agape,
So for me it's more love to come,
My walk is to be like God's Son,
Love has brought me this far,
I reflect sitting in the pews,
The tabernacle listening to the man of God,
The holy one, my vision is sharp,
Releasing my thoughts,
I need David to come play his harp,
I'm taking the biblical course,
Trying to come closer to the truth,
Trying to correct my mistakes,
Time to increase my faith,
Time to elevate and relate as I patiently wait,
Not ashamed to let the tears dry on my face,
I am here through His saving grace,
Look down at the footprints in the sand,
I was carried through, it was one set of footprints
now it's two, guide me as I walk by your side,
Let your Word abide, let me recognize your plan,
So I cannot be stopped,
Foundation, here I stand on the rock

Simple Life

Whenever I fall to the world, I tell myself
I have to get back to the simple life,
No worries of material things,

Do I have water?

Yes

Do I have food?

Yes,

Do have shelter?

Yes...

Let me stay focus on the goodness of what I have,
let me live more simple,
So I can help more people in need,
Limit any desires of greed,
Fill my heart with helping those that are lacking,
Let me put this plan into action,
The simple life will translate into relaxing.
Simple life is my new fashion

Spiritual Message On My Wrist

Simple creation of expression
Set through my foundation
Revealed to enhance my lifestyle,
Which I hope to inspire others to be who they are,
The 14 karat gold is to separate its uniqueness
From what others might try to duplicate,
Really my skin is sensitive to other metals,
The first piece is sand dollar,
Which represents to teach faith as the five holes
represent the wounds Christ endured.
The center blooms the Easter Lily
With the star of Bethlehem,
The next piece is the dove
To show there is always hope
Of all that believe in Him,
Call his name and safety will overtake you,
When I was stranded in the sea,
His presence was there,
The next piece is the cross,
Reminds me of the sacrifice of Jesus
And for me to sacrifice for others,
The last piece the guardian angel,
I know God has placed one or some in my life,
The overall message of the bracelet is simple,
I'm a child of God

The Mind

From the Mind, the Pen, and the Paper,
To the Mind to Microsoft Word,
New method continues for the Mind to IPhoneNotes
All different methods but the same approach,
Deliver what God shared through this gift,
Express my goals and if I had one wish,
It would be to be who HE called me to be,
You can see my growth like the rings in a tree…
Expressing my truth so I can be truly free,
7 books will make this a completion

The Struggle

When I opened up the Word,
It gave me strength when I was lost,
It gave me love and support,
It gave me the words to keep my on course,
I focused on the light,
My faith grew and my blessings did too,
Through my struggle,
I pushed through the rubble,
I went to the Word when I was in trouble,
Through heartache and misery,
It showed the Christ in me,
I was healed again, and like real men,
I cried, I weep, tears of joy,
I'm back on my feet,
The strength to overcome, thy will be done,
Thank you Jesus

There is room

There is room for improvement
There is room for guidance
There is room for forgiveness
There is room for sharing
There is room for growth
There is room for empowerment
There is room for being taught
There is room for me to be better

What do I do?

What do I do with this energy?
What do I do with these suggestions?
What do I do with these opinions?
What do I do with these disagreements?
What do I do with this conflict?
What do I do with these plans?
What do I do with these feelings?
What do I do with this disappointment?
What do I do...
I simply hand it over to God

Wonderful 9:59 a.m.

What I am trying to say…
It may have took me some time
But I finally got it right this time,
I know exactly what to say
And I can see all that I have
Flaws and all, I believe in love
And it's time to give my all
Yes, I may have been holding back
At our first encounter and through the years,
However, that is not the case
Now as I see the light beam in my face,
I must stand for love and give it my all,
This is where I belong,
I believe through every hopelessness,
Given up or suffering,
HE has shown me love can conquer all
And I want to give all my love to you

Zenith

Something about blue,
It is my foundation as I learn more about You,
The creator of the stars,
I look far in the distance,
My thoughts tell me it's a Virgo thing,
The hues of blue,
The sapphire that explains I'm the earth
You are my birth,
You separated the darkness from the light,
As I reflect on when my life is dark
The light is winning with one spectacle of a twinkle
As I see through a wrinkle in time,
Its time after time the light prevails,
Something about blue has a story to tell,
It's simple, be calm the light will appear

87

Average Cost of new house $92,000
Average income per year $24,350
Average monthly rent $395
Average Price for new car $10,355
Gallon of Gas $0.89
US Postage Stamp $0.24
Ronald Reagan is President of the United States

Michael Jackson releases the "Bad" album
Whitney Houston releases the "Whitney" album
George Michael releases the "Faith" album
Gregory Abbott releases "Shake You Down" single

Movie "The Untouchables" is released
Movie "The Witches of Eastwick" is released
Movie "The Princess Bride" is released
Movie "Predator" is released
Movie "Can't Buy Me Love" is released

Friday July 31, 1987
The Baptism of Marcus Yates Ford
A Child of God
Proverbs 22:6

Majestic Forte
Marcus Yates Ford
Foundation 2019

Signature
2020

www.ingramcontent.com/pod-product-compliance
Lightning Source LLC
Chambersburg PA
CBHW070510090426
42735CB00012B/2721